What Would You Do?

THE CALIFORNIA GOLD RUSH

Would You Go for the Gold?

Elaine Landau

Enslow Elementary

an imprint of

Enslow Publishers, Inc.

40 Industrial Road
Box 398
Berkeley Heights, NJ 07922
USA

http://www.enslow.com

Enslow Elementary, an imprint of Enslow Publishers, Inc.

Enslow Elementary® is a registered trademark of Enslow Publishers, Inc.

Library of Congress Cataloging-in-Publication Data

Landau, Elaine.
    The California Gold Rush : would you go for the gold? / Elaine Landau.
        p. cm. — (What would you do?)
    Includes bibliographical references and index.
    Summary: "Discusses the California Gold Rush in American history, including the first discovery of gold, the
        49ers, and how the gold rush changed the landscape of America"—Provided by publisher.
    ISBN-13: 978-0-7660-2901-9
    ISBN-10: 0-7660-2901-8
    1. California—Gold discoveries—Juvenile literature. 2. California—History—1846–1850—Juvenile
        literature. 3. Pioneers—California—History—19th century—Juvenile literature. 4. Gold miners—
        California—History—19th century—Juvenile literature. 5. Frontier and pioneer life—California—
        Juvenile literature. I. Title. II. Series.
    F865.L25 2008
    979.4'04—dc22

                2007038455

Printed in the United States of America

10 9 8 7 6 5 4 3 2 1

Illustration Credits: Associated Press, pp. 5, 6 (top), 18, 21, 26 (jeans), 42; Bancroft Library, p. 6 (bottom); The Bancroft Library, University of California, Berkeley, pp. 29, 32, 36; The Bridgeman Art Library , pp. 10, 22; California State Library , p. 33; Enslow Publishers, Inc., pp. 4, 8; Getty Images, p. 31; The Granger Collection, New York, pp. 19, 23, 25, 26 (miners), 28, 37, 38, 40; © 2007 Jupiterimages Corporation, pp. 1, 17, 41, 43 (bottom), 45 (top); Library of Congress, pp. 9, 12, 13, 14, 16, 20, 30, 34, 43 (top), 45 (bottom); North Wind Picture Archives, pp. 27, 35; North Wind Picture Archives/Alamy, p. 11.

Cover Illustrations: The Granger Collection, New York.

CONTENTS

GOLD IS DISCOVERED!

Can you guess the most exciting day in California history? Some say it was January 24, 1848. Gold was found that day by James Marshall in a river near a saw mill.

Gold Rush Sites

California
Rich Bar
Bidwell's Bar
Mormon Island
Sutter's Mill/ Coloma
SACRAMENTO
Weber's Creek
OAKLAND
Murphy's
SAN FRANCISCO
SAN JOSE
Mariposa
Pacific Ocean
Comstock Lode
Nevada

It happened on John Sutter's land. Marshall found a few gold **nuggets** in the American River. Then a few days later, more nuggets were spotted.

Sutter's Mill was located near the present-day city of Sacramento. This and other places where gold was found are marked by gold bars on the map.

Tourists walk around a replica of Sutter's Mill, where gold was discovered by James Marshall in 1848.

All the pieces were tested. Those shiny stones were really gold! California would never be the same.

Sutter did not want anyone to know about the gold. He did not want strangers on his land. He thought that treasure hunters might try to dig there after dark. But his secret was too big to keep.

This gold nugget (right) is thought to have started the California Gold Rush in 1848. It is about the size of a quarter.

This ad used a picture of gold miners to try to get people to sail on a ship to California.

Soon word of the discovery spread. Newspapers ran stories about it. People were excited by the news.

They dreamed of getting rich quickly. Some eagerly believed all sorts of stories. Many thought that California's hills and rivers were filled with gold.

Gold fever swept through California. By 1849, it had spread to the East. Even people in far-off countries heard about it. They dreamed of finding gold in California, too.

WHAT WOULD YOU DO?

What if you lived in the East in 1849? *Would you . . .*

* Be willing to take a risk? Would you pack your bags and go west?

PEOPLE MOVE WEST

People headed west in large numbers. Farmers left their farms. Shopkeepers closed their shops. Soldiers moved west to become miners. Sailors did the same as soon as their ships docked.

The largest group of people headed for California in 1849. They became known as 49ers because of the year they moved. Americans were not

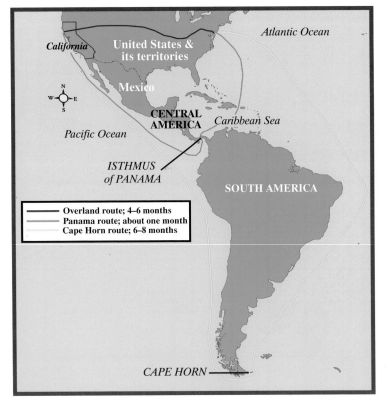

There were three main ways that people could get to California.

8

the only ones heading to California. There were people from Chile, Sweden, France, China, and other countries, too.

Getting to California from the eastern United States was not easy. Some people went by ship. Many ships set sail from eastern seaports. They sailed around the tip of South America. From there, they went up the Pacific coast to California.

Sailing around Cape Horn, at the southern tip of South America, was the longest route to California. The seas around Cape Horn were often very rough.

The owners of this ship used a picture of a flying fish to show how fast they could get gold seekers to California during the Gold Rush.

The trip could take over six months. Ship captains often charged very high prices and packed their vessels with passengers. As many as three men might share a bed. Some did not even have a bed.

The food often spoiled at sea. Sometimes it was filled with bugs. The stale water tasted terrible, too.

There was another sea route to California as well. Would-be miners sailed through the Caribbean Sea to Panama. There they crossed a thin strip of land known as the **Isthmus** of Panama. When they reached the Pacific Ocean a second ship would take them north to California.

But the ships going north with room for extra passengers did not come very often. Sometimes gold seekers waited for months.

Crossing the Isthmus of Panama was also not easy. Fortune hunters had to travel through **swamps**. Many of the men caught **malaria**—a tropical disease carried by mosquitoes. They died before they ever reached California.

A ship drops off passengers at the Chagres River, on the Caribbean coast of Panama. The miners had to travel across Panama to the Pacific Ocean to catch another ship to California.

There was a land route to California too. The trip from the East coast to California was about three thousand miles. Hopeful miners headed west by horse, mule, and ox-drawn wagons. Others even made the trip by foot.

It was a long trip through rugged areas. Some became trapped in the Rocky Mountains once the snows set in. Some of these people starved to death.

In other places, there were long stretches of desert. Some gold seekers and their animals died of thirst there.

WHAT WOULD YOU DO?

✳ What if you decided to go west? You are not sure which route to take. Can you guess what most people did?

MANY TRAVELED BY LAND

Many 49ers took the land route to California. They thought it would be quicker. Many also did not have a lot of money. They could not afford to pay the high prices ship captains wanted.

Before long, miners were not the only ones taking the land route west. Others went west and joined them on these trails. **Homesteaders** and ranchers came to start farms and raise cattle.

People would travel over land to California in wagon trains. These wagon trains were long lines of wagons. People traveled together for protection.

Sometimes, the traveling miners would kill buffalo and not use all the meat from the animal. American Indians thought this was a waste. They believed that most of the animal should be used for food, clothing, or tools.

However, one group was not pleased with this westward movement. This group was the American Indians. The new settlers and gold seekers were taking over the land.

American Indians had always depended on the buffalo for food. Yet before long, the newcomers killed off most of the buffalo. Many Indians went hungry. They wondered if they would survive as a people.

People moving west brought diseases that the American Indians quickly caught. It was harder for them to fight off these diseases. Many of them died.

Those heading west on wagon trains had feared American Indian attacks. Yet early on, this was not much of a problem. The real enemy was a deadly disease known as **cholera**.

The white settlers had brought cholera west with them. Many on the wagon trains died of it. The Indians were hit especially hard by the disease. Their bodies were not used to the disease the whites carried. Sometimes whole Indian villages were wiped out.

WHAT WOULD YOU DO?

What if you were an American Indian? *Would you . . .*

✳ **Carry out raids against the white people? You want to save your people and your way of life.**

✳ **Try to get along with the white people? They are probably here to stay.**

AMERICAN INDIANS FIGHT AND WORK

Some American Indians fought to save their land. However, it was a losing battle. The white people were better armed. There were more of them, too.

Other American Indians agreed to work for the whites. Miners sometimes hired them to **pan for gold**. Often they worked long hours for very little pay. A miner might give an Indian a shirt for a pound of gold. Meanwhile, the whites who hired the Indians became rich.

A white man chases an American Indian on horseback. White settlers and American Indians often fought each other because of their differences.

Panning for gold took a long time. Doing it all day left the miners in a lot of pain. They often did not find any gold.

Nevertheless, things were not going well for many miners. As it turned out, only the first ones there had gotten rich quickly. By mid-1849, most of the surface gold was gone.

Yet many miners still panned for gold in the rivers and streams. Panning for gold was hard, backbreaking work. To do it, the men had to squat in cold water for hours.

The miners scooped the mud from beneath the water into a shallow pan. Then they moved the water around in the pan. This allowed the dirt to wash over the pan's side. Gold is heavier than dirt, so gold would be left in the pan.

Miners spent whole days doing this. All the while, their hands and arms were under cold water. Often their fingers went numb.

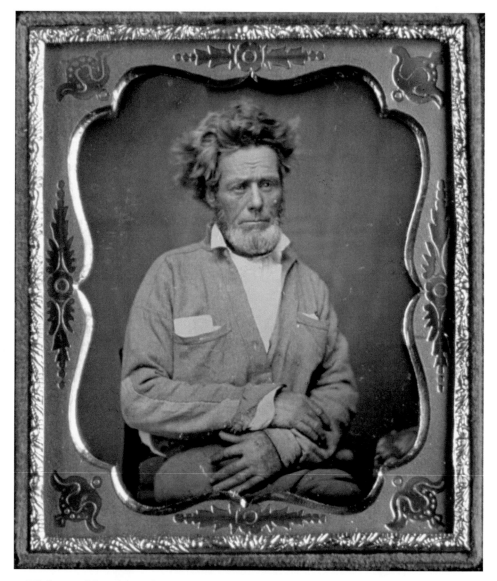

This gold miner has swollen hands from panning for gold in cold water for such a long time.

Despite often not finding any gold, many miners kept trying their luck.

Their dreams of becoming rich soon ended. Their pans were never filled with large gold nuggets. They settled for panning gold dust or gold flakes out of the water. It was barely enough to keep them going.

Others headed for the hills to look for gold. There they dug long tunnels. At times these tunnels collapsed. Such cave-ins killed many miners.

By about 1850, machinery began to replace digging and panning. Machines let miners reach the untouched deposits of gold far beneath the surface. Yet teams of men were needed to work the equipment.

At first, these men worked together in small groups. Then in the early 1850s, large mining companies moved in.

sluice

Gold miners shovel sand from a stream into a sluice. A sluice was a container used for finding gold in a large amount of sand from a stream.

During the 1850s, large companies began to take over much of the mining in California.

They could afford better equipment. They took over most of the area's mining.

Miners had to accept the truth. It was now much harder to get rich without help from others.

WHAT WOULD YOU DO?

What if you were a miner? You went west to become rich. Now that does not look likely. *Would you . . .*

* **Work for a company? As a hired hand you will not make much money, but at least you will get paid.**

* **Keep mining for gold on your own? You have come a long way and will not give up your dream of riches.**

MEN JOIN MINING COMPANIES

Some miners refused to give up their dreams. They kept looking for gold on their own. Very few did well.

By about 1851, many had put their hopes aside. They did not want to starve. These men finally accepted jobs with large mining companies.

The mining season lasted from about May to November. Winter in the mountains could be brutal. The temperature often dropped below freezing. There were heavy snows, too.

A gold miner holds his tools for a photo that he sent back home to his family.

Men look for gold near mountains in California.

Most miners left the hills for the winter. However, some kept mining. They did not want to waste any time. They wanted to send money back to their families.

Staying in the hills during winter could be dangerous. Once heavy snows began, people could not use the roads. Food and supplies could not be brought to mining sites. Some miners starved, while others froze to death.

Early spring in the hills was risky as well. Often heavy rains went on for days. Roads were washed out as rivers overflowed. Some miners drowned.

WHAT WOULD YOU DO?

What if you were a miner? Your family in the East needs money badly. *Would you . . .*

* **Risk staying in the mountains through the winter to work?**

MINERS TAKE RISKS, OTHERS GET RICH

Most miners stopped working in the winter. Yet some took a chance and stayed in the mountains. At times, these men made it through the winter safely. However, there were some accidents. Miners often died in these accidents.

Many of those who became rich during the Gold Rush were not miners. These men were not about to spend a freezing winter in the mountains. Instead, they were merchants who supplied the miners with what they needed. Since there were not many stores, miners often paid very high prices for supplies.

During the Gold Rush, a single egg cost between three and five dollars. In 1850, three dollars was equal to about seventy-five dollars today. So that was quite a costly egg!

An apple was a dollar, while a pound of butter went for

During the Gold Rush, mining towns filled with people. By 1852, Columbia, California, had grown into a large community.

six dollars. One can of sardines could cost as much as sixteen dollars.

Some California merchants heard that would-be miners heading west were dying of thirst on the trail. They went out to the desert areas with barrels of water. There, drinks of water sold from one dollar to one hundred dollars.

Sam Brannan became rich during the Gold Rush. Early on, he bought up every shovel, pick, axe, and pan around.

Levi Strauss sold jeans to miners in California. Above, workers at the La Grange Mine near Weaverville, California, wear Levi Strauss jeans in 1880. Levi jeans (upper left) were found in 1996 in an abandoned mine. They are thought to be over one hundred years old.

Sam Brannan made a lot of money by selling tools to the gold miners in California.

He knew that miners would need these things. He paid less than a quarter for each pan but sold them for nearly twenty dollars each.

Other merchants did well during the Gold Rush too. Levi Strauss made sturdy canvas pants for the miners known as "Levis." Levi jeans are still popular today.

WHAT WOULD YOU DO?

What if you were a merchant in the early 1850s? You are doing well, but you are hardly rich. *Would you . . .*

✳ **Take a chance and head west?**

MERCHANTS TRY HARD AS THE CHINESE ARRIVE

While some merchants went west, most did not. Getting rich was not a sure thing. Not every merchant did well.

Americans were not the only ones who went to California. People from other nations came as well. Some hoped to sell things, while others sought gold.

By 1852, there were 25,000 Chinese people in California.

A Chinese immigrant makes his way to the California gold mines.

Chinese travel to San Francisco, California, on the steamship *Alaska*.

Chinese gold miners often set up camps where they slept in tents.

Yet as gold became harder to find, things became harder for them. Many Americans did not want them there.

Americans wanted whatever riches were left to go to themselves. In 1850, a foreign miner's tax was passed. Under this law, miners from other countries had to pay a tax.

Things became even worse for the Chinese. Soon they were not allowed in mining camps. Chinese miners could only work land that the Americans had left.

Chinese workers pan for gold in California.

But, Chinese miners worked hard and found gold in places that other miners had left. This made the Americans even angrier. At times, they chased the Chinese off these claims. They kept all the gold for themselves.

Some American miners turned to violence. They beat up the Chinese miners. A number of Chinese were even killed.

WHAT WOULD YOU DO?

What if you were a Chinese miner in the early 1850s? You do not feel safe mining any longer.

Would you . . .
* ✳ **Go back to China?**
* ✳ **Come up with another way to do well in California?**

THE CHINESE AND WOMEN FIND A WAY

Many Chinese stayed in America. They found different ways to earn money. Some opened laundries. This was a service the miners needed badly. Others cooked for the miners.

Like the Chinese, women were another group that struggled to find a place in the

Chinese miners were often pushed off their land by white miners. Many Chinese decided to make money other ways. At the left is a Chinese grocery store and butcher shop.

Some women made money by selling food to miners. At the right, a woman brings lunch to three workers.

Gold Rush. The few women who came to California were usually the wives of merchants or miners. Women also worked in the **saloons**, of which there were hundreds.

However, other women did what the Chinese did. Some opened businesses. They offered services the miners really needed. Like the Chinese, they cooked meals for the miners and did their laundry. A few even had barbershops. They gave the miners haircuts.

WHAT WOULD YOU DO?

What if you were a woman working in a factory in the East? You want to earn more. *Would you . . .*

✳ **Leave for California?**

ONLY SOME WOMEN GO TO CALIFORNIA

A few women went west and did well. However, people frowned on women going west during the Gold Rush. Mining towns were wild and lawless. They were thought to be no place for a woman because they were so dangerous.

Butte City, California, quickly grew into a large mining town.

California became a state on September 9, 1850. People hoped that would calm things down. Yet statehood did not bring law and order to the area right away.

Whenever a large deposit of gold was

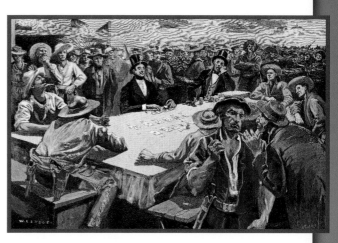

Gold miners in a saloon play a card game called faro.

found, men flocked to the area. Mining camps quickly sprang up. If the claim turned out to be real, these grew into **boomtowns**, towns that filled with people quickly.

The boomtowns had names like Suckertown and Helltown. These towns often had a saloon and a gambling house. Most were open twenty-four hours a day. Many miners spent what little money they had there.

When in town, miners often drank. At times, tempers flared. Arguments were usually settled with guns.

Nevertheless, these dangers did not keep all women away. Some were determined to become successful.

WHAT WOULD YOU DO?

What if you were in a boomtown? You have met some others who want to bring law and order to town. *Would you . . .*

✳ **Join this group?**

35

MINERS FORM GROUPS TO FIGHT CRIME

There were no police or jails in mining towns. Groups of people called **vigilantes** tried to do the job. Such groups may have started out to fight crime. However, they could be as scary as the criminals.

These gunmen were part of a vigilante group in California during the Gold Rush.

This picture shows California vigilantes in the 1850s.

Sam Whittaker and Robert McKenzie were hung by vigilantes in San Francisco in August 1851.

These groups did not set up real courts of law. If most of the people in town felt a man was guilty, then he was. Justice was swift. Someone could be put on trial in the morning and hanged by noon.

Lawyers defending those accused were sometimes afraid to speak up. The people at these "trials" could be very angry. At times, they attacked lawyers who tried to defend those accused. The lawyers feared for their own lives.

The same was true for witnesses. Sometimes the angry crowd just wanted a hanging. They did not want to hear from witnesses. If the vigilantes believed the person was guilty, that was enough for them.

Hanging was common for those guilty of murder and serious theft. There were other punishments too. Those guilty of crimes were sometimes **branded** with hot irons. Others were whipped.

WHAT WOULD YOU DO?

What if you were a miner who did not like this type of justice? You also do not want to live in a dangerous boomtown. You have not made your fortune yet. *Would you . . .*

* ✳ **Pack up and go home?**

MANY HEAD HOME AFTER THE RUSH

Lots of men went home. Others tried to stay as long as they could. They did not want to go back empty-handed.

The Pilgrim rejoiceth ober his "Pile."

Going home poor meant that they had failed. This was hard for many miners to accept.

Some only stayed long enough to make enough money to go home. To do this, they often had to work for a mining company for over a year. During this time there

A miner is happy because he found gold. This picture went with a poem called "The Miner's Progress, or Scenes in the Life of California," published in 1853.

Many miners went to California, hoping to find gold nuggets or even gold dust in the region's streams and rivers.

was often little extra money to send back to their families.

Every so often, someone would strike it rich. For a short time, everyone's spirits would soar. They would remember the days before 1850. Back then, some miners made over a hundred dollars a day. Before all the surface gold was taken, riches seemed to be everywhere. Thinking of the past, the miners' old dream suddenly seemed possible again. Yet for most of them, it remained just a dream.

WHAT WOULD YOU DO?

✳ **What if you were a historian? You have been asked to take a close look at the California Gold Rush. What do you think it meant for the country?**

THE GOLD RUSH HELPED AMERICA GROW EVEN MORE

Many people have studied the California Gold Rush. They agree that it was an important time in America. Not every person discovered gold. Yet the country became richer and more united because of it.

Some miners actually did find gold. These gold bars from California were found in the wreckage of a ship that sunk off the coast of Central America.

San Francisco was a small coastal town (top) at the time of the Gold Rush. However, it soon grew into a bustling city because of all the people that moved west. Today, it is one of the biggest cities in California (bottom).

Thousands did not go back. They stayed in the unsettled area between Kansas and California. They built towns and did well as merchants, farmers, and ranchers.

These areas later became states. They added to America's wealth. The gold that was discovered in California boosted Americans' riches as well. After the Gold Rush, America was never the same. It grew stronger and better than ever.

TIMELINE

1848—*January 24*: Gold is discovered in the American River near Sutter's Mill.

1849—The largest group of people goes to California seeking gold. They are called 49ers.

1850—Miners begin using machines to reach gold; large mining companies open for business in California; a foreign miner's tax is passed.
September 9: California becomes a state.

1851—Many miners begin accepting jobs with mining companies.

1852—By this year, the Gold Rush had brought twenty-five thousand Chinese immigrants to California.

WORDS TO KNOW

boomtown—A town that fills with a lot of people quickly.

branded—Having a mark burned into a person's or animal's skin.

cholera—A serious illness that can result in death.

historian—A person who studies people or events from the past.

homesteader—A person who had a farm in the West.

isthmus—A narrow strip of land that connects two larger masses of land.

malaria—A tropical disease carried by mosquitoes.

nuggets—Small lumps of gold.

panning for gold—A method in which miners would shake pans filled with water, clay, rocks, gravel, and perhaps gold, from the bottoms of rivers and streams. Gold is heavier than the other material, so it settles on the bottom of the pan.

saloon—A bar where alcohol is sold; the saloons were also meetinghouses.

swamp—An area where the ground always contains a lot of water.

vigilante—A person who catches and punishes people who are believed to be criminals; a vigilante is not a police officer and does not give a person a fair trial.

LEARN MORE

Books

Blashfield, Jean F. *The California Gold Rush.* Minneapolis, Minn.: Compass Point Books, 2001.

Doeden, Matt. *John Sutter and the California Gold Rush.* Mankato, Minn.: Capstone Press, 2006.

Dolan, Edward F. *The California Gold Rush.* Tarrytown, N.Y.: Benchmark Books, 2002.

Schanzer, Rosalyn. *Gold Fever!: Tales From the California Gold Rush.* Washington, D.C.: National Geographic Children's Books, 2007.

Internet Addresses

Experience Gold Rush!
<www.museumca.org/goldrush>
This Web site takes you back to the days of the Gold Rush. You will see and hear wonderful stories about that exciting period in our history.

PBS Kids Go! Gold Rush
<www.pbskids.org/wayback/goldrush/>
Visit this Web site for some great information on the journey of the 49ers and much more.

INDEX